ENTREPRENEUR?
WORKBOOK
Bring Your Vision to Life

A 25 day journey for Christian entrepreneurs

Ralph McCall

destinée

Copyright © 2011 by Ralph McCall

This workbook is a condensed version of 'Entrepreneur? Bring Your Vision to Life", 2006 and 2011.

Without limiting the rights under copyright reserved above, no part of this publication may be reproduced, stored in, or introduced into a retrieval system, or transmitted in any form or by any means (electronic, mechanical, photocopying, or otherwise), without the prior written permission from the publisher, except where permitted by law, and except in the case of brief quotations embodied in critical articles and reviews. For information, write: info@destinee.ch

Reasonable care has been taken to trace original sources and copyright holders for any quotations appearing in this book. Should any attribution be found to be incorrect or incomplete, the publisher welcomes written documentation supporting correction for subsequent printing.

All scripture quotations, unless otherwise indicated, are taken from the HOLY BIBLE, NEW INTERNATIONAL VERSION®. NIV®. Copyright ©1973, 1978, 1984 by International Bible Society. Used by permission of Zondervan. All rights reserved.

Published by Destinée Media, www.destineemedia.com

Cover concept: Per-Ole Lind
Cover image: psdGraphics

All rights reserved by the author.

ISBN 978-0-9832768-2-1

Table of Contents

Introduction: Bringing Your Vision to Life   1
Day 1: You are a vision builder, an entrepreneur   3

Action One: Identify Your Vision
Day 2: What is your vision?   4
Day 3: Search within yourself   6
Day 4: The pressures that may stop you   7
Day 5: Your vision: Is it worth it?   9
Day 6: Goals and age groups   10
Day 7: Your story   12
Day 8: Vision and faith   14
Day 9: Reframing your vision   16

Action Two: Establish Your Map
Day 10: The Map Maker   17
Day 11: Your Plan   18
Day 12: Domain—Who and What?   19
Day 13: Compass—Where?   20
Day 14: Tools and choosing them—How?   21
Day 15: There is a bottom line   22
Day 16: Money: From Where?   24

Action Three: Manage the Stages with Wisdom
Day 17: Setting the Stage(s)   26
Day 18: Essentials for Tasking   28

Action Four: Set and Achieve Targets
Day 19: Targets and dates   30

Action Five: Be Accountable
Day 20: Confide and consult   31
Day 21: Keep your secrets   32

Action Six: Take Action
Day 22: Act now!   34

Action Seven: Get the Spiritual Implications
Day 23: Distinctive service   36
Day 24: In the spirit   38

Conclusion
Day 25: Sum it Up   39
Into the journey   40

About the Author   41

INTRODUCTION: BRINGING YOUR VISION TO LIFE

In the midst of all personal and economic circumstances it is possible, with God's leading, to achieve an entrepreneurial idea. To bring your vision to life it means you need to define it, put a plan in place and then take the necessary actions to make it happen. And it involves faith. That is the process outlined in this book.

Entrepreneurs come in many forms, but to be one most often starts by asking the question that begins, "What if . . . ?" For instance:

What if I started a new ministry through my church? Or a new humanitarian work?

What if I started a new business such as manufacturing a product? Or, providing a service?

What if I did something about the needs of my family, or needs I see in the world?

For a destitute family of nine in a Manila shanty town, the question began when the parents asked themselves: What if we could provide education for our children? They put all of their energy into helping their oldest son through law school. He in turn supported his next sibling through university, and together they helped the rest of the children complete degrees.

This was one simple form of an entrepreneurial act, at a family level. It started with "What if?" and turned into reality.

One interesting thing about being an entrepreneur is that the "What if?" can be asked at a multitude of different levels, from the individual, to the family, to the neighborhood, to the city, state and world. It can cover everything from people, products and services; every aspect of the world around us, spiritually, socially, economically.

We all have these "What if?" dreams. It is a God-given part of our nature. It is to imagine and create. It is to restore the world and make it better.

What is your vision?
What are your dreams and desires? What are your recurring imaginings or wishes of how things could be that, if fulfilled, would make a significant difference in your life and the lives of others? These lead us to your vision.

Articulating your vision is often difficult, but if you can identify your deepest, God-given desires, narrow them down to their essence, and plan for their realization, you can bring them to life.

One of the tasks God asks of all people is to tend to the world and make it better. It is to participate with him in his redemption for the world. It starts with spiritual redemption through believing in Jesus Christ and his salvation. It continues as we bring the Lordship of Christ into every area of the world around us.

Every person on this planet has a *general calling* to live lives of faith in God and to daily walk with Him. And, every person also has a *distinctive calling*. God has created us as individuals with unique capabilities and interests. Therefore, God can give us unique ideas, or visions, of how the world around us might be changed and be made better for His glory. Unfortunately many people don't believe and follow that general calling, nor do they understand their distinctive calling.

Without a vision the people perish
Proverbs 29:18 states quite bluntly that "Without a vision the people perish."(KJV). As in: no vision equals death. Visions are not just pleasant mental images to keep life interesting during a long commute. They are necessary for life.

What exactly is a vision? We will expand this later, but for now look at vision as *a vivid mental picture and goal for how things can and should be.* Vision is a passion that drives you forward and gives your life and actions both purpose and meaning.

Workbook Purpose

What is your vision? Simple enough question, but can you answer it this second, in a couple of sentences?

The purpose of this workbook is to help you state your vision and work through bringing it to life. When you are finished, you should be able to actively pursue an endeavor that will bring a positive change to the world around you.

The concepts in this workbook are explained in greater detail in the book, *Entrepreneur? Bring Your Vision to Life,* ISBN 978-0-9759082-9-7, published by Destinée Media; wwwdestineemedia.com. Please reference the full book for a more extended view. At the same time, the workbook has all the basics for enabling you to move forward with your vision.

This workbook is written for Christian entrepreneurs, although the fundamentals found in this book are relevant for anyone embarking on an entrepreneurial venture.

Using the Workbook

The next statement is extremely important as you progress through this book:

Deeply reflect on each question to get the most out of this workbook.

Don't skip any of the questions. Don't rush it. Don't do more than one chapter each day. Reflect on each question during the day, or over many days if necessary.

This is serious business. It is the business of vision-building.

Now, are you ready to articulate your vision and see it realized? Are you ready to be an entrepreneur?

DAY 1: YOU ARE A VISION-BUILDER, AN ENTREPRENEUR

Let's start with the word 'entrepreneur.' Many people stumble over this word and feel it does not relate to them or their vision. You might be surprised. Take a minute to answer the following questions:

1. When you think about the word 'entrepreneur' or 'entrepreneurship,' what do you think of? What are entrepreneurs to you? What are their characteristics? What are their qualities?

2. Do you think of yourself as an entrepreneur?

Reflect on the following definition

Entrepreneurship is the process of identifying, developing, and bringing a vision to life. The vision may be an innovative idea, an opportunity, or simply a better way to do something. The Entrepreneurship Center at Miami University of Ohio

In universities the term 'entrepreneur' is no longer just focused on the aspect of starting a new commercial enterprise. Yes, that is still relevant, but now people also speak of social entrepreneurship. They also speak of political entrepreneurship, when you change the political system. And starting a new ministry is entrepreneurship.

The *innovative idea, opportunity, or simply better way to do something* in the above definition most often has to do with making the world a better place, in some way. The world is a fallen order and we need innovative ideas to improve it.

We need innovation in the commercial world to change and advance it. Personal relationships often need better ways of doing things. The environment requires new techniques to better conserve it and improve its use. The political world needs new ways of doing things. The opportunities for entrepreneurship are enormous.

Building a vision is an innovative activity with the purpose of redeeming and advancing.

#

We are called to be agents for positive change. To be vision-builders. Once you begin the process of identifying, developing and bringing a vision to life, you have in fact become an entrepreneur.

Questions:

1:1 Seen within this context, ask yourself the questions from the opening of this chapter again: Do you see yourself as an entrepreneur? Do you see yourself as an agent for positive change? Do you see something that needs to be changed? Do you see opportunities for better ways of doing something?

Spend a day thinking about this. What would you like to change in the world? Maybe it's something personal, or with your family or friends. Maybe it's broader, like something that needs to be made better in your town or at your workplace. As you go through your day, think about opportunities for change. Try and imagine and think outside the box. Make sure you write down your thoughts in your notebook. The purpose of this is to get your imagination working, to prepare for *identifying, developing and bringing a vision to life.*

Action One ▶
Identify your Vision

DAY 2: **WHAT IS YOUR VISION?**

Before you answer the question of what your vision is, make sure you fully understand what we mean when using the word "vision."

A vivid mental picture
Dictionaries define vision as something exceptional. To paraphrase Merriam Webster, vision is:

1. **A religious or mystical experience of a supernatural experience**
2. **The act or power of seeing or imagination**
3. **A vivid mental image**

One gets motivated to think of vision along these lines. Here you find the focus on things mystical and supernatural.

A vision is a vivid mental picture born in your imagination. It elevates us toward a grander purpose in our lives.

An ecstatic beholding
To truly understand the meaning of vision, it is helpful to see how the word is used in the Bible. The most frequent usage occurring in the Old Testament is the Hebrew word, Hazon חזון, which translates to 'an ecstatic beholding by the seer.' As the Proverb mentioned earlier told us, "Where there is no vision *(hazon)* the people perish." So that could read, "Where there is no *ecstatic beholding by the seer*, the people perish."

Vision also arises in the context of divine revelation and appearance.

Many companies have 'vision statements' that are nothing more than a dry set of objectives to be met in three years time. An ecstatic beholding is something different and much more motivational.

You must be passionate about your vision and not treat it like another idea to be broken down into a master plan. While the vision may indeed involve planning, note that its origin will be a vibrant experience, an imagination, a vivid mental image. This is what will motivate you to carry it through.

Origins of a Vision

The origins of entrepreneurial visions are as diverse as society itself. If you feel blocked when trying to imagine what your vision might be, consider the following starting points for visions.

You might:

- **Have an idea for new products or services**
- **See the need for a new process or better way of doing something**
- **See the needs of others**
- **Notice that changes are needed in the institutions you are a part of**
- **Envision opportunities of various kinds**
- **Seek to improve relationships amidst family, friends, community, or nations**
- **Realize your own personal interests and needs**
- **Acknowledge the need for a personal change**

Your world is full of opportunities of all kinds at all levels. But there is likely one thing that will stand out from the rest, one that you would love to spend an entire day doing. It might already be nudging you to pay attention to it. Now you are ready to begin identifying it.

Here is a question that might seem strange or out of place. In fact, it provides a starting point. The purpose of this question is to help you get in touch with yourself; especially with the things you enjoy doing. It is to get your creativity working, for you will need a lot of imagination and creativity in the following chapters.

Just brainstorm and imagine.

Question:

2:1 Can you envision your ideal day? What does it look like from waking to sleeping? Think about your needs, capabilities and desires. What kinds of work activities do you enjoy doing the most? What about recreation? What would that ideal day look like if you had to do it again and again? Be as specific as you can. Don't worry if it sounds silly or serious, impossible or simple. What would you spend an ideal day doing?

Spend time reflecting on this. Make sure that you write the answer in a notebook, as well as the answers to all the questions in the following chapters.

DAY 3: SEARCH WITHIN YOURSELF

Whether you are nine or ninety you can have a vision that you feel passionately about, a vision that pulls you forward. It's like having a goal you can't resist moving toward.

Start by searching within yourself

One good starting point for identifying your vision is to begin by taking a good look at yourself. As you reflect on these questions, write down your answers in your notebook. There are a lot of questions here and it may take longer than a day to go through them. Don't rush it. Take your time. Think through each one:

- What am I most passionate about?
- What am I good at?
- What are my core competencies?
- What can I be the best at? (Not what do I wish to be the best at)
- What is my personality: introvert, extrovert?
- What do I enjoy doing?
- Where do I see need in the world around me?
- What is it that I really want to do?

In the process of answering these questions, it is important to submit your search to God, involving his insight and direct leading. Ultimately what you're after is what you are called to do. Your calling can be difficult to recognize because it's closely tied to your identity — knowing who you are, how you define yourself, and your unique qualities.

Your vision is already there

Your vision has likely been waiting in your heart for some time. It is an idea that you continually keep coming back to. Your vision may already be there, but for various reasons, it has been marginalized and needs to be recalled. But know that the process of achieving that vision may involve your attention over months or years. That's a small investment for changing the course of your life. So begin searching for possibly dormant desires already residing in your soul.

Questions:

3:10 What are your dreams or visions? Write whatever comes to your mind: things that you strongly feel should happen, the things you dream, things you want changed. Put aside for now suggestions that family and friends have made.

3:11 What is your most important vision? Go through your list. Remember that a vision is a vivid mental picture of how things could be for you and others in the future. Which vivid picture holds the most importance in your life?

3:12 Draft a vision statement: In fifty words or less, write the first draft of your vision. You will probably be reworking it in subsequent chapters, so don't worry about getting it perfect.

3:13 What is stopping you from achieving your vision? Make a list of the things that are keeping you from achieving that vision.

DAY 4: **THE PRESSURES THAT MAY STOP YOU**

In the last chapter you began to identify your vision. One question also asked the things that are holding you back from achieving it. Let's think about things that might stop you.

Your vision is outside your normal boundaries: Keep in mind that your vision often places you in entirely new territory, outside your normal routines.

You need to be willing to take risks and step outside existing boundaries. You need to "think outside the box" and then move outside it.

 The rat race and daily grind: Your life is filled with daily demands and challenges. Once one problem is solves, another seems to pop up.
    The ancient Greeks understood this. The mythological character Sisyphus got to spend eternity pushing a rock up a hill only to have it roll back down. And then he had to push it up again.
    Daily responsibilities and pressures need to get done. But they can hinder you from moving forward to achieve your vision by demanding all of your energy.

The corporate ladder: In the work world, you may be caught up in trying to advance to a new position, "climbing the corporate ladder". Or, it may be just hanging onto your rung by meeting a stack of new objectives your boss handed you.

 Society's pressures: Then there are the social systems. These may be written or unwritten rules that establish constraints about what you 'should' and 'shouldn't' do. If you come up with a new idea, those around you may call you or your idea crazy. Social systems around you can be resistant to the changes brought by your vision.

Thought processes: You also have to face the doubts and fears in your own head. Everyone has those internal gears grinding, "I can never do that, I shouldn't take the risk, I'm going to fail, I don't know what the outcome is really going to be," and so on. Don't underestimate the power of those recurrent negative messages that may even sound legitimate. Negativity keeps you from stepping out and going after that vision.

Multiple ideas: Often we can have many ideas at the same time. This can be part of the creativity process. The problem is that one idea replaces another, which replaces another, ad infinitum. Nothing ever really gets done. Or if it does, it doesn't fit a more comprehensive theme in your life.

So your vision sits out there, but one or all of the dynamics above might be holding you back from achieving it. It's important to realize that these constraints are at work all the time.

If you don't identify the ones in your own life and deal with them, you will not be able to bring your vision to life.

Questions:

4: 1 Which of the above constraints (or others) weighs most heavily in your life and why?

4:2 Are there other constraints that may hinder you in achieving your vision?

4:3 Specifically what can you do to overcome these constraints?

DAY 5: YOUR VISION: IS IT WORTH IT?

Run your vision through a seven-question filter, for two reasons. One is to determine your vision's merit. Two is to help you understand your real motivations.

Questions:

5:1 Does your vision provide a service and how?
A janitor, a banker and a homemaker all provide valuable services. Service is evident in most work activities. What is the service component in your vision? How will your vision deliver that service? Identify this and your motivation will increase.

5:2 Does your vision redeem?
God is the great redeemer and we are called to follow him. Does your vision somehow better the world? Specifically, how and where does your vision redeem?

5:3 Does your vision fit your gifting?
Do you truly understand your personal characteristics, interests, special skills and capabilities? What energizes you, and how do you respond to a broken world? If your gifting does not fit your vision, you may end up being dissatisfied.

5:4 Is your vision realistic?
Unfortunately for many people, their vision is only an illusion. You run from idea to idea with initial high hopes, then hit a barrier and bang and the dream is over. Ask yourself: is your vision one of these illusions? Or is it actually achievable?

5:5 What are your true motivations for pursuing this vision?
"Selfless" acts can make us feel good about ourselves, and sometimes "selfish" ones can benefit others. Get all of your motivations on the table and be uncompromisingly honest with yourself. What are your *true* motivations for pursuing this vision?

5:6 What are the relational implications?
Most visions have social repercussions because they will impact relationships—family, friends, colleagues, etc. Some of these people may accept and support what you want to do while others will not. Your vision is also likely to open up relationships with new people. Ask yourself: what are the relational implications of my vision?

5:7 What are the economic implications?
God created an economic reality that is interwoven into this world. Your vision, no matter what it is, possesses economic impact. The economic implications may be small or big. How much financing is needed and where will it come from?

DAY 6: GOALS AND AGE GROUPS

Let's address an area that may give you a bit of perspective. Vision applies to everyone, but everyone owns a different set of experiences through which they will build their vision. And those experiences vary depending on what age you are.

To generalize things, just say that our adult lives are made up of three phases:

Phase One
This applies to young adults who are in university or just getting started in their careers. It might be difficult to realize a goal at seventy-one, but it's probably harder at twenty-one. When students in their late teens or early twenties are asked, "what is your vision?" their answer is usually a blank stare. Here are a few potential reasons why.

There is the burden of pressures mentioned in an earlier chapter. Pressures to get an education, get a job, and to be what the immediate social system expects you to be. When you enter your twenties, you move beyond the academic routine of the education system and become more independent. Then all of a sudden you are faced with figuring out what you want to do with the rest of your life.

And the options may be innumerable. If you choose one you can't have the others. And, if you choose one, what happens if it turns out to be the wrong choice? Stalemate.

Then there's the struggle with identity. They don't know themselves selves well enough to answer.

For anyone of any age — but especially for those still figuring out who they are — it's advised against picking vision goals that are too grand for your present circumstances or are too idealistic. That can be a recipe for failure.

If you have a big vision, break it down into small actions that you can accomplish. My advice to vision-seekers in this age group is to try and find one thing that truly interests and excites you and that you can achieve in a short period of time. This may be linked to a longer-term goal, and accomplishing it will help you learn about yourself. With some experience under your belt, you can move forward to the larger visions. Take it one step at a time.

Phase Two
In this age group, you often have enough life experience to be able to say, "this is who I am, this is what I feel is important, and this is what I want to do."

You also have a huge burden of responsibility, and to survive it you establish routines. Routines can be life-saving, but they can also be difficult to break. You start becoming part of the system rather than looking for positive ways to change it.

But being in the system can work to your advantage. It allows you to see opportunities for starting new ventures in your company, getting involved in ministries at your church, or initiating humanitarian projects.

To do these things, you need to be in charge of your routines instead of letting them be in charge of you. Carve out regular times away from your daily demands to think through the things you want to accomplish sooner and later.

The advice here is to identify some small but significant short-term goal that fits on the continuum leading to that longer-term vision. Take manageable actions toward what you ultimately desire to accomplish.

Phase Three
Somewhere in this phase we may enter something called "retirement". It's uncertain exactly what this is. If a Christian's basic job description is to have faith in God, and to redeem the world

and make it better, then this activity is not something that stops when we become sixty-five. It is a life long activity.

This phase is actually a time of life when many people have good health, financial security and a wealth of knowledge and experience to bring to the world. We can certainly slow down and have some fun, but let's be careful of thinking that's all we are called to do.

If you are in this phase, the advice is to purposely look for needs around you. And then meet these needs. Find something that interests you. You have knowledge, experience and some capital to make a difference.

Don't just live for your own pleasure. Instead, think in terms of *the one last important thing I can do to make the world better*? What is it? This is your last chance.

#

At every age, consider: a) an understanding of the needs in your own life, b) an understanding of the needs in the world, and c) your response to these needs.

Questions:

6:1 What phase are you in? How will the realities of being in that phase impact you as you pursue your vision?

6:2 What are the needs and desires in your own life and how do you respond to them? Your needs might be such things as personal aspirations, emotional healing, spiritual development, or generally betterment.

6:3 How do you perceive the needs and desires in the world and how do you respond to them?

#

This is a check to make sure you are taking your time in answering the questions. Hopefully it is requiring serious thought. While the chapters are broken down as "Days", it is okay if you take more than a day on any question.

And, make sure you are writing your answers in a notebook. You should be going back to your answers and revising them as you think more about them. Also, you will need your answers for an exercise in Day 24.

DAY 7: **YOUR STORY**

At this point, you have hopefully identified your vision and determined that it is valuable and worth pursuing. Now you make it happen. To do that, it helps to see your new adventure in the context of a 'narrative', a story. If you understand the key components of narrative, this may help you be better prepared for some of the dynamics you will encounter.

The journey of bringing your vision to life is an adventure. Some day you will be able to look back at the entire process and share it with others by saying, "Here is my story."

Your journey is an adventure story

Perhaps you haven't thought of the vision-builder in terms of narrative before. When you begin to read a story, you usually meet the main character, the protagonist. And then something happens that launches that hero or heroine into the unknown on a quest to reach a goal, whether physical, emotional or spiritual.

This is the timeless setup: "Once upon a time something happened." In fact, that describes your entrepreneurial project. Once upon a time something happened. You got this idea and you stepped out into the unknown on a quest.

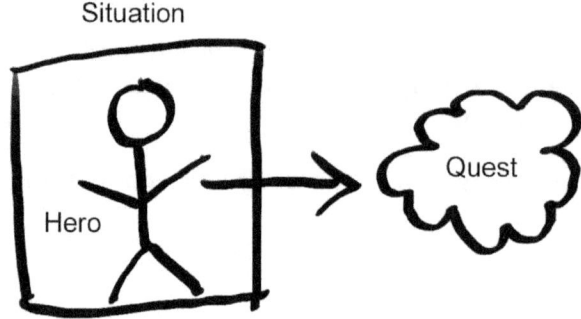

The question is, are you really going to take that action? Many people stay in their current situation because they are afraid of the risk. Are you going to remain in fear or step out into the unknown?

Stepping into the unknown forest

Stories are adventures. Stories start by stepping into the proverbial forest. It is not coincidental that many of Grimm's fairy tales take place in a forest. The dense, dark wooded space is an illustration of the unknown. You come to the edge of a thick forest, and you can't see where the path will take you.

But that is how your story begins. If you truly feel passionate about your vision, you will step into the forest. Like the protagonists in most good stories, you have something serious at stake — your vision.

The thing about your vision is that often it's outside of yourself. It's something that you've never done before. And in almost all cases, it exists outside your normal, probably comfortable, life patterns.

Know your enemies
When you have a protagonist, you usually have at least one antagonist as well. The 'bad guy.' But he/she/it can be harder to identify in a vision quest, because your antagonist isn't always a person. It could be a concept, a fear, or even a destructive pattern in the main character's mind.

Know that your antagonist will try to stop you from achieving your quest. Therefore it is important that you know the enemies in your life.

Character development
Following your passion will present you with many challenges. How you respond to those challenges will enable you to learn, to grow and mature: character development.

Most of you can look back at a rough experience in your past and see that you grew and learned despite the difficulty or even pain involved. So hang in there when things get hard.

#

Remember that your entrepreneurial story is your individual adventure. You get to decide whether to step into the forest, whether to know and prepare for your enemies once inside, and whether to face challenges or give in to fear.

Think about your story.

Once upon a time . . . .

Questions:

7:1 What or who are your enemies that will stop you from achieving your vision? In an earlier chapter, you examined what was stopping you from achieving your vision. Revisit this and see if anything else has occurred to you. It is important to know your enemies so that you can answer the next question:

7:2 How are you going to deal with your enemies? Now that you know your enemies, how are you doing to conquer them? Do you have any "combat" strategies in place? If not, develop a battle plan here.

DAY 8: VISION AND FAITH

There are two ways to enter the forest. Either you step forward entirely on your own, or you engage God in your endeavor.

Are you on your own?
The materialist paradigm essentially says that the material world is all there is. Therefore, if I want to achieve anything in this world, I need to learn to manipulate the material reality.

As Francis Schaeffer explained in *The God Who Is There*, one way to see the world is as a 'closed system'. There is nothing other than energy and matter. What you see is all there is. From this, when you attempt to achieve a vision, you do so from your own resources, starting from and depending purely on yourself.

This view may initially seem attractive, to be the rugged, individual hero facing challenges solo. Maybe in theory. Maybe, but when standing face to face with the dragon, it's much better when you have a helping hand.

The unseen reality
For the Christian, reality consists of both the seen and the unseen: an 'open system.' It is more than what we can see, touch and manipulate. An open system allows for interaction between the spiritual world and the physical world. This allows you to see both the process of realizing your vision and the process of achieving your vision within a much broader framework than the materialist.

Within the 'open system' way of seeing the world, one finds a multitude of spiritualities. But the Christian view is quite different from all the rest. It starts from the position of a loving, faithful and all-powerful God who has created the heavens and the earth, who exists and is present in his creation. Because of the original fall in the Garden of Eden and each person's failure to achieve God's perfection and holiness, humans were separated from him.

God offers a solution to that separation: his Son. Christ is the one and only mediator between humans and God. Through the working of the Holy Spirit in our lives and by accepting what God has done for us, we can become spiritually redeemed. And that redemption can work its way out into redeeming the brokenness of all the areas of the world around us.

The Christian also holds that God is engaged in his creation. That fact directly relates to your vision and your pursuit of it, because God is the one who provides you with the visionary idea, and he walks with you through the journey of achieving it. He provides you with courage and insight as you step into the unknown forest. He is the one I want with me when I face each "dragon."

Not all visions come from God. This is a broken world with fallen people who can have broken visions. There are many examples of great political, commercial and religious visions that have ended up hurting people.

Test your vision out with God. Pray, meditate on his word, and seek wise council. The following diagram shows how God is the covering for your vision as a vision-building story. He is engaged from beginning to end:

Engage the Lord
Unfortunately many Christians operate from a dual reality. On Sunday they go to church, pray and worship God. The rest of the week they act as materialists in a closed system, doing everything on their own strength as though the spiritual world were nonexistent. The more consistent Biblical perspective is that God is involved *at all times*. He isn't just with you on Sunday mornings.

If you believe in a spiritual world, then you recognize that God is involved in your current situation. You understand that he has placed a vision in your heart and given you the competency to bring it to life. You know that he will enter with you into the unknown forest and will empower you to face your enemies. And you know, even as hard as it can be, that he will use these circumstances to develop your character.

This is the life of faith: trusting God and engaging him at every action of the journey.

Question:

8:1 How does your vision fit into your spirituality? How is God involved in the origin and initiation of your vision idea? How will you engage with God as you go on your vision-building journey, facing the unknowns in the forest and confronting your enemies?

DAY 9: REFRAMING YOUR VISION

With the foundational concepts in the last few chapters in your mind, revisit your vision statement. Anything to tweak, change, overhaul?

If your vision doesn't inspire you, you won't be inspired to bring it to life
Remember that your vision statement is not a plan. It is where you want to go. Your quest. If your written statement sounds flat, rewrite it until it takes on a special meaning to you and you can't wait to make it happen.

Your vision statement will typically be a short phrase that may contain any or all of the following components:

It isn't status quo: Your vision differs from what currently exists. It is a quest for something new. Things are going to change if you bring it to life.

It is future-oriented: Because your vision will be something new, it is future-oriented. That means that it contains a picture—either explicitly or implicitly—of how things will be in the future. Your vision statement may or may not include a sense of timing.

It matters: Doing what matters revs your motivation dramatically. Your vision should capture the potential of a better, redeemed reality on a spiritual, social, economic, or ecological level.

It is active: Your vision should contain a sense of movement. Think of verbs like: grow, change, provide, bring, lead. These express action and transformation.

It is based on a fundamental belief: Your beliefs will and should pervade all areas of your life, especially your vision.

Essentially, your vision statement should express the destination you are headed in a way that builds your commitment.

Question:

9:1 Using some or all of the components listed above, rewrite your vision in a way that captures both the importance of what you are doing and the passion you feel for it. Keep it to around fifty words or less.

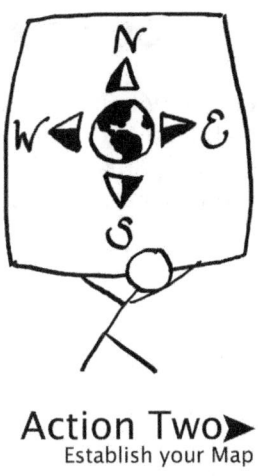

Action Two ▶
Establish your Map

DAY 10: **THE MAP MAKER**

You are the cartographer. You draw a map for this journey. To make your idea happen, you have to allocate time and resources to laying it out. Your vision won't happen unless you make it happen.

That means you need a strategy. In his book *Strategy Safari,* Henry Mintzberg groups strategy into two different types: strategy as a forward-looking plan and strategy as internal patterns.

Strategy as a forward-looking plan
With this strategy, you look into the future and build targets, actions, and dates into a cohesive structure. Then you set key priorities, milestones, and allocation of responsibilities, the essentials to following through with your vision. A topic covered in the next chapters.

Strategy as internal patterns
Whether or not your vision comes to life is intricately knotted to your existing patterns of behavior. "Strategy as internal patterns" involves knowing what patterns work for you and changing the ones that don't. As you know, changing internal patterns can be extremely difficult.

If you have a problem making time for new projects, ask yourself what unnecessary activities can be time-limited, or even eliminated entirely. Change your existing patterns. If you don't, you are unlikely to bring your vision to life.

Learning to say no and setting priorities are difficult processes. You have to make hard choices. When you are truly passionate about a vision, you minimize activities that don't contribute. You make constant choices to focus on the path that will lead toward your goal. If you deviate into non-vision activities, you are quick to realize it and immediately take corrective action to redirect yourself.

Getting rid of disruptive and irrelevant patterns can be dramatic and difficult. Think about where you are now spending your time and what needs to be eliminated.

Questions:

10:1 What are the major milestones you need to meet in order to achieve your entrepreneurial vision? We will deal with this in more detail in further sections.

10:2 Examine the patterns of behavior and routines in your life. Which ones will stop you from achieving your vision? And, how will you deal with them?

DAY 11: YOUR PLAN

As you saw in the last chapter, you need strategy to manage the patterns of behavior in your life. Now you turn to drafting a strategic plan, the other essential aspect of strategy.

Instead of sending you off to draft pages of plans, the following pages will simply guide you through the essential things you need to consider and to introduce you to the questions you will be answering for your vision.

Be flexible

None of the tactics in your plan are set in stone. Business leaders make both tactical plans and contingency or scenario plans. A contingency plan considers flexible approaches for achieving their tactical plan. Establish your plan and tactics, but remember that once you enter the unknown forest you need to be prepared to make modifications. You never know what might cross your path.

Definition creep

One large danger in planning is called 'definition creep.' This is when you start piling more and more details or functionality onto your basic definition, your vision statement. It starts with saying, "Wouldn't it be great if we added this? Oh, and let's add this. And wouldn't this also be nice?" You start gluing on so many bells and whistles that the vision isn't even visible anymore.

Definition creep can happen at the beginning of a project, and it can happen after you are well under way. In all cases, stay away from definition creep. I advise keeping your vision to one clear concept and keeping your plans simple and extremely focused on that one concept. Definition creep can kill the project.

Keep it simple and focused on the absolute essentials.

Key factors to establish your map

In the following three chapters, you will answer difficult questions that are essential for grounding your vision. It will involve hard work. Before progressing, answer the following:

Questions:

11:1 Keeping flexible planning in mind, write out what might happen if your vision is a huge success, a static endeavor, or a huge failure.

11:2 What are your plans in each scenario? What implications are there for you in each scenario?

DAY 12: DOMAIN—WHO AND WHAT?

The first item in putting together your plan concerns domain. Domain encompasses the product or service you will provide and the people who will be using it (recipients), and it covers your communication plan.

Questions:

12:1 What is the specific product of your vision?
Every vision has a product or service embedded within it. That 'product' is a specific thing or service that will benefit your recipients. Ask yourself of your vision, "Specifically, what is my product and exactly who will be using it?" Keep in mind that the word 'product' also applies to services, but if you don't like those words, then substitute it with 'offer'.

12:2 Who are the recipients of your vision?
Who will benefit from your vision? And where will they benefit from it? Whether you are starting a new company or a non-profit organization, you must ask, who exactly are your recipients? Can you describe them by demographics, as well as specific economic characteristics?

By understanding this information, you will be prepared to make good decisions while implementing your plan. You will know where to focus your efforts. If you incorrectly define your target recipients, then you will be wasting time.

12:3 What is your communication plan?
People will be impacted by your vision. If you are producing a product or service, you need to inform your market about it and to explain its benefits. How will you communicate with those potential recipients? How will you make them aware of the product offering or the change resulting from your vision?

12:4 Is there competition?
Do some research and find out if someone else is offering similar products or services. If so, you will face competition and may be vying for the same resources. Or you could join forces with the competition and work together. You need to compare the relative strengths and weakness of your own offering, which in turn will help you identify niche areas where you will succeed. Who else is doing the same thing and how does that impact you?

DAY 13: PLACE - WHERE?

Your vision will remain in the realm of your imagination until it becomes grounded in reality. You need to define in great detail where you will produce your product or service, how will you produce it, and how will you get it to your user/customer.

Questions:

13: 1 Where will you produce your product?
Be as specific as you can in where you will produce your product. Ideally, you should be able to name a town and even a building. By naming the place of activity or production it brings your vision into reality, into physical bricks and mortar. The place where you produce your product or service is likely to change over time. Where will your initial production take place, and where might it be happening in the future?

13: 2 How will you produce it?
There are a myriad of ways to do things. Your production process may simply be you working on your own personal computer at home. Or your production process may involve the delegation of duties to a staff in a building designated for the use of distributing your vision product.

If you have a commercial venture, you will probably need to work with suppliers, and when it comes to manufacturing your product you may not want to do everything on your own. Therefore you may want to outsource certain aspects of the production.

When you begin to think about the production of your product, remember that there is always more than one way. Think about your different alternatives. Don't immediately lock yourself into one method, but also don't keep your options open indefinitely. Start with one mode of production and work from there. Evolve this over time.

13: 3 How will you get it to your recipients?
Once your product is ready, ask yourself how you will supply it to your recipients. In the case of products, think about how orders will be taken and processed. In the case of services, how to make them available and where will they be delivered? Will you meet with people face-to-face or will you have intermediaries who deliver your service? In the case of a physical product, how will you distribute it to your recipients? People not only need to know about your offering, but they also need to know how to obtain it.

DAY 14: **TOOLS AND CHOOSING THEM – HOW?**

This concerns the organizational and administrative part of your vision. Here are some very important questions. Think about each one of them:

Questions:

14:1 What's your entrepreneurial vision's organizational structure? Who makes decisions? Who is accountable to whom? What are the essential tasks to be performed?

14:2 What kind of resources do you need and when? This should cover everything from computers to accounting.

14:3 How many, if any, staff will you need now and in the future?

14:4 What kind of network of people will you need?

14:5 Who are your key contacts? (Translation: who do you know?)

14:6 What associations should you join now?

14:7 What educational institutions should you link up with?

14:8 What kind of support system do/will you have outside your own organization?

14:9 What's your legal structure? Most entrepreneurial visions, commercial or not, will involve the creation of some kind of organization. If so, then early in the process, decide how you want to be legally structured. Will your vision end up a one-person show, a partnership, an association, a not-for-profit, or something that involves shareholders? This enables you to open a bank account. Each alternative involve tax implications? How are you impacted?

14:10 Who do you need as partners, investors, volunteers? And what agreements are needed? Other people are likely to be involved in your venture. Get everybody's expectations out on the table. Choose people you know you can work well with (friends sometimes make terrible business partners). Write down—don't just discuss—what kind of work the participants will be doing, and in what capacity you will work together. Don't forget to address how people will be remunerated. Without getting things specified it opens the door for conflict. You'll have enough obstacles to face without that. Sit down with those involved, pray for God's guidance in the discussion, and get it on paper.

DAY 15: THERE IS A BOTTOM LINE

Let's step aside for a moment and think about money in a spiritual context. Money is everywhere. You can't escape it, especially when you are bringing a vision to life. It is important to acknowledge that there is a financial reality. The bottom line is: there is a bottom line.

Many visions go astray because of poor financial understanding and neglectful management of economic realities. This is often the case in the Christian world, where views and attitudes towards money can get rather peculiar. Do any of these sound familiar?

View #1: Bankrolling God
There are some Christian entrepreneurs who up-front state that they are carrying out their project to make "tons of money" to give away to Christian works. There is nothing wrong in giving money away to Christian works. In fact, the Bible has many references that command believers to support widows and orphans and to help the poor. The problem here is the focus on making 'tons' of money. This can defocus the vision builder from effectively managing the visionary process. The vision loses importance while the money-making gains importance — even becoming the new focus.

View #2: The Reward Model
Another view with Christian entrepreneurs is what one might call 'The Reward Model' which says "If I do something of value to God, then God will financially reward me." This attitude shifts your emphasis away from wisely managing a project for its own value to doing it only because you await God's financial reward. Remember, God is not a puppet.

This attitude might say such things as, "If I walk in the spirit then God will bless me financially." Or: "If I support social causes, or start a new company, or am absolutely holy, or if I evangelize . . . then I will receive a financial reward."

Besides being a weak theology, this view robs your vision of its inherent importance as a creative and redeeming action in the world. That importance itself — God-given as it is — should be where your passion for the vision quest originates. Not from the "reward money" you have decided God will give you.

View #3: 'Faithalistic' finances
The 'faithalistic' view is fatalism disguised as faith. The logic behind it goes something like this: "No matter what I do, God will provide." Yes, in the Bible you can see that God is the great provider. Yes he is there and he supports his people. But he also expects you to do your share of "tending to" things. God is God and generally it seems he does not expect you to passively sit back and wait for manna from heaven. Doing so is telling God what he will do for you — the wrong attitude to base your actions (or inaction) upon.

This *faithlistic* attitude leads you to do your job in a sloppy fashion because, "God will cover for me." This affects your attitude about how money is managed. It says "I don't have to pay attention to all that, because God can pick up my slack with miracles." This produces inattentiveness to, and even mismanagement of, your funds.

This so called "faith" should never be used as a cover for laziness, sloppiness, and wasteful living. Are you going to choose fatalism or faith?

The economic reality: get your foundation solid
The preceding views toward money fail because we live in an economic reality along with a spiritual, ecological, social reality, etc. You can see this economic reality via these foundational principles:

1. Spirituality is an earthly reality The spiritual world is not separate from the physical world. In his book *'On the Way'* Gordon Smith writes: "Spirituality encompasses the whole of life. True spirituality is not otherworldly; rather, it enables us to be fully in the world." God is concerned with every area of reality, both the seen and the unseen. Our task is to bring his lordship into every area of reality and not just relegate it to church on Sunday and a few other 'spiritual' things. Spirituality encompasses all realms of life including the economic realm.

2. Human acts usually have a financial component In *Godly Materialism*, John Schneider writes: "All the great acts of God were economic events." From Genesis to Revelation, The Bible is clear that economics are part of God's reality.

3. Economics are congruent with God's principles As you work to achieve your vision, you engage God in the process *he* started in your heart. It follows that the financial aspects of your vision need to be congruent with God's principles. Your vision is hardly beneath God's dignity and concern; neither are the finances.

The teachings and acts of Christ are centered on redemption. First and foremost is the redemption of bringing fallen individuals back to God – the restoring of relationship. In addition you see his redemption in all other areas including economic redemption.

#

Christ taught about the dangers of wealth, yet also the importance of managing it with wisdom. As you work to achieve your vision, keep your view of finances and financial management congruent with God's principles of economic management.

Questions:

5:1 What is your worldview concerning money and God? Think of the three 'attitudes' listed above. Do you fit any of these?

5:2 Examine your financial relationship to God and your expectations of him. How does this practically work into the realities of your entrepreneurial venture?

DAY 16: MONEY – FROM WHERE?

Unless you win the lottery or come into a surprise inheritance today, you have to find funding to support your vision. If you can already bankroll the first actions or even the complete process of your vision, you still have to manage your money wisely.

Start by answering the following three questions. Note that though they look simple, they require some effort now and even more later:

Questions:

16:1 What money is needed?
Notice that the question implies two parts: the beginning and the ongoing. Do not neglect either part, because each will have different complexities. Many initial expenses may not recur, whereas downstream, you may have regular periodic costs such as salaries, rent, fees, etc. How much will it cost you to get your vision going—what are your start-up costs? And once you have begun, how much will it cost to keep your vision going?

You need to realistically address the financial reality of your vision.

16:2 Where will the money come from now and later?
Where will you get the money to get started? Without the assurance of that funding, your project is unlikely to come to life. And just getting the startup funding isn't enough. Additional phases will require funding. Your funding model may change throughout the life of your entrepreneurial endeavor. Exactly, where will the money come from at each phase?

16:3 Are you covered? If not, what are you going to do about it?
Will your vision create enough revenue to cover your expenses? If not, what will you do? Once you know your overall financial requirements and where the funding is coming from, you need to know if there will be enough money to cover your expenses. If not, then you have a problem and need to solve it. In business terms, you need to figure out your break-even point: the point at which the funding will cover your costs.

Does the way you are spending your money reflect your vision priorities? If you tend to spend irresponsibly or neglect your financial circumstances, watch out. Continuing with poor money management habits will endanger the birth, let alone the life of your vision.

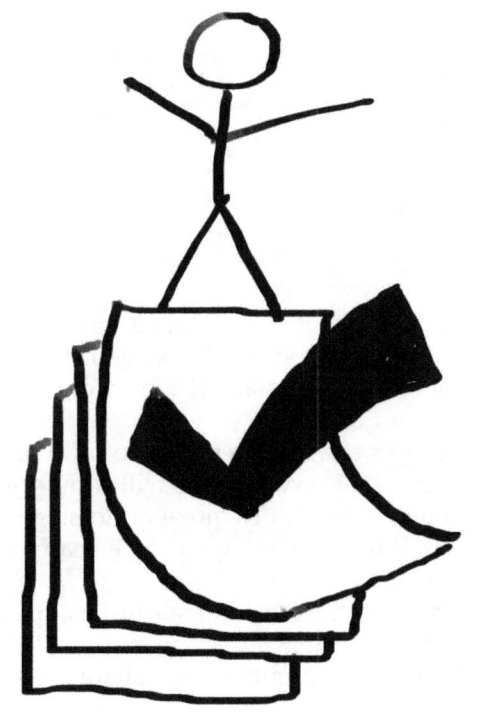

Action Three ▶
Manage the Stages with Wisdom

DAY 17: SETTING THE STAGE(S)

Every entrepreneurial endeavor goes through four stages. It is important to know what stage you are in and to complete that stage before moving on to the next. The stages are as follows:

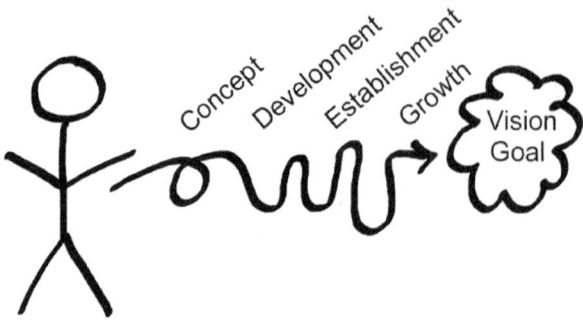

Stage One: Concept
This stage is where your vision concept is developed, not only on paper, but also practically. If your goal were to build a physical product, this stage involves building a prototype to see if it actually works. It means getting specific about who would be using that product. It's about managing the construction of your concept.

Here you also test your concept — Alpha testing. Get it to other people, such as experts and potential recipients of your product or service. This will allow you to reach the milestone of stage one: proof of principle. This means you only move on to stage two if the experts or recipients agree that your idea has merit. If they do not agree, listen carefully as to why, and then go back and make necessary adjustments.

The risk level is highest here. In the world of startup companies, the concept stage is where you face the greatest difficulty in raising money from outside investors. If venture capitalists come in at this stage, they know the enormous risk. Therefore they will ask for a large stake in the equity of the endeavor.

Stage Two: Development
Now you get to assemble the infrastructure to support your vision. In this stage, you bring your concept into reality. That's why you need infrastructure and the flexibility to change it as it makes contact with reality. Don't move forward and expand if you have major adjustments to make. The milestone of the development stage is acceptance by your recipients. People who invest in your vision at this stage will still be expecting a high equity stake, or ownership.

For those of you starting humanitarian or social projects, you will often find individuals with a strong interest in your vision.

At Stage Two is it is often easier to find people willing to give money philanthropically.

The risk level starts to decline in this stage. Though the development stage often requires the most groundwork for establishing initial infrastructure, it has moved beyond the point of pure concept. You are now implementing your idea in the real world and demonstrating its validity.

Stage Three: Establishment
In this stage you are establishing your concept. Stage two required select acceptance by test recipients, stage three requires general acceptance by your target recipients.

The key milestone here is general acceptance by your target market. That means there are people who want your product or service. If your vision is commercial, your milestone is 'Invoice #001'. If it is a humanitarian or social project, your milestone is when the target recipients are benefiting from your service and donors have agreed to provide the ongoing funding to keep your organization running.

The risk level in this stage begins to drop. Your vision idea has started to prove itself. It is succeeding.

Stage Four: Growth

The growth stage takes on an entirely different complexity. Here, you have brought your vision to life. Now it is a matter of keeping it alive. To do this, you need to develop and establish an enduring infrastructure for the following: 1) Processes, 2) Organization, 3) Management, 4) Production, 5) Market development, and 6) Product/Service enhancement.

In this stage your key milestone is viability of the endeavor. This goes beyond breaking even or even making a profit: you have brought your vision to life and now you get to build that vision and/or move on to something new.

Your risk level has dramatically decreased. If your vision was a commercial endeavor, it will begin to command the highest return on investment. If your vision is non-commercial, its structure is up and running, or you have come to the end of your quest and ready to use this as a stepping-stone to the next journey.

#

You cannot sidestep these stages. Manage them wisely and carefully. Remember to focus on each key objective and milestone while keeping the next stage in mind.

Questions:

17:1 What stage is your entrepreneurial project in? Detail your current focus, milestone and funding source.

17:2 What is the next major milestone you need to achieve that will allow you to move onto the next stage? Be as exact as possible.

DAY 18: **ESSENTIALS FOR TASKING**

You could view the stages in the last chapter something like this:

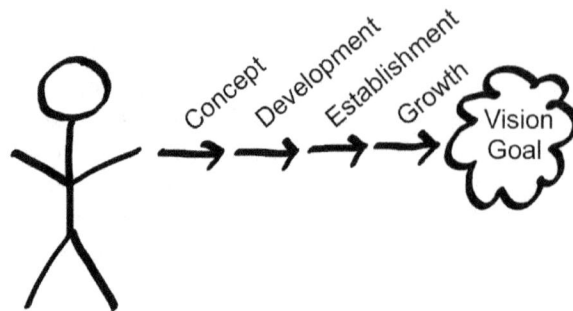

Each stage needs to be broken down into a series of actions or tasks in order to achieve your milestone. Simpler visions may involve only one or two tasks in each stage, while more complex visions might involve dozens. To assist with that process, here are some ideas for managing whatever tasks arise in your vision.

Guess or test?
Unless you are a Biblical prophet, any projections you make into the future are on a best-guess basis. The specific plans you make (tasks) in each stage are your approximation of what it will take to move your vision project forward.

In the context of starting new ventures, if objectives don't work, then set new oness and try again. Consider it hypothesis testing. In other words, to bring your vision into reality, you may have to backtrack and tweak things. While your plans may be carefully made, it is not set in stone. If necessary, modify and retrace your actions.

Ready, set, step . . . in faith
On the surface, it might seem discouraging to operate from a best-guess standpoint. But when you do, you are in fact stepping forward in faith into the unknown. In life, if you knew exactly what to do and exactly what to expect, you wouldn't need much faith. It's the same in implementing a vision—or any other endeavor.

Now the question is: what do you put your faith in? Is that task purely a material manipulation of facts and objects, or does it engage God? Where and in what is your faith as you move through each task and stage?

Align your resources before each task
Know what resources you need before beginning each task. Your ideal situation is to have those necessary resources in place and aligned before you even begin a task. But don't be surprised to look back and see that some "essentials" you invested in turned out to be useless. As I've said, you can't predict the future.

Get funding plus buffers
How much funding will you need for each stage and each task within it? Should you raise enough money to cover the entire project, or just enough to cover the next action? It is recommended to

raise enough money to cover the next action or phase. As each project stage succeeds, it becomes easier to engage more investors if needed. And with each successful stage, you have the chance to think through the best funding model—which may not be evident when you begin the project. Still, don't wait too long to raise money. It takes time. Think ahead.

Consider outsourcing
To stay focused on the essential success factors in your project, it is suggested to consider outsourcing. Pay someone else to do non-critical tasks. The money you spend is actually an investment in your vision, because it frees time for the essential tasks within the stages of your vision. At each stage examine the necessary tasks and see what someone else can do.

Are you getting carried away?
In many entrepreneurial projects there is a decision-making blunder that might be called 'the expediency of the moment.' It happens when you make short-term decisions without adequately thinking about the long-term needs of your vision project.

Expediency-of-the-moment issues arise in all arenas. It may be the need for that special piece of equipment, which is not needed in a few weeks time. It may be moving into a place you don't need, or engaging people at the wrong time.

The problem is that the 'need' of the moment can take on an entire life of its own. Some people treat each need as supreme, neglecting to think about its long-term impact. They go from need to need, moment by moment.

As you move through the stages from task to task, remember that each action is a small part of your larger vision. Take your time, stand back from each perceived need and balance it against the long-term requirements of your endeavor. Don't be led astray by the expediency of the moment.

Questions:

18:1 Go back and reflect on your answers to last chapter's questions. What stage are you in? What are the specific tasks required to achieve the major milestone you have set for that stage?

18:2 What is the very next task you need to accomplish?

Action Four▶
Set and Achieve Targets

DAY 19: TARGETS AND DATES

Set targets for each major milestone with the following components.

Tasks
Tasks are things you need to do to achieve a milestone. They are quantitative and measurable. You could say Michael's task was to get to the airport on time to catch a specific flight. Targets support your vision.

Dates
To further quantify the target you need to set some dates and timelines. If you have put a schedule in place, when will each action within the schedule take place? What is the final deadline for attaining that task or reaching the milestone for the phase?

Responsibility
A final aspect of a good target is the person responsible for achieving it. If you don't assign responsibilities, then tasks can fall between the cracks. That means they won't happen on time, if at all.

Don't let that happen.

Questions:

19:1 Establish a set of tasks that will enable you to achieve the objectives for the phase you are in.

19: 2 Are your tasks measurable? If not can you redefine them to be so?

19:3 By what exact dates will you accomplish your tasks? And, who is responsible for achieving each task?

Action Five ▶
Be Accountable

DAY 20: **CONFIDE AND CONSULT**

Why be accountable to someone? For all the reasons you've read thus far; because your journey will have its ups and downs, because you will have to address the pressures and enemies working against you, because of your existing patterns of behavior, because your motivation level will fluctuate.

Even though you are more or less your own "boss" on your visionary journey, it is extremely helpful to be accountable to someone. This confidant should, as the name implies, be someone you can confide in. Your vision project is about you, and as you progress through it, you will discover things about yourself. When you find yourself stumbling through weaknesses and struggles, it helps to know that someone is there to listen and even advise.

So the role not only involves confiding, but consulting. Choose someone you know is able to carefully listen and help you see things from a different angle. You need someone to ask the hard questions.

Once you find your 'consultant,' agree to meet regularly. Schedule the days and times in a calendar.

And when you have successfully brought your vision to life, treat your consultant to something special.

Question:

20:1 Who will you be accountable to?

Once you've answered that question, Day 21 is founded on a wise proverb that will enable you to protect your entrepreneurial idea.

DAY 21: KEEP YOUR SECRETS

"Beware before you share!"
Your vision belongs to you. Be careful about sharing it with anyone, and be careful about when you release your information. Here are some reasons:

Someone can steal your idea
People copy good ideas and you never know what someone will do with yours. In the business world you have a Non-Disclosure Agreement or 'NDA.' With this agreement, one party consents to not disclose information that the other party has shared with them—information usually related to products or a business plan. Have people sign a NDA before you share too many confidential details. If your vision is not commercial, still be very careful. Other people can steal your idea.

Your credability is at risk
When you share your vision, you expose yourself. People immediately have expectations of you. But what if your vision needs further refinement? Don't expose yourself too soon, for your credibility is at risk.

Information overload damages your vision
Be careful how you release the information on your vision. Don't tell everything all at once if you don't have to. If you need to persuade people to gain their commitment, drip them information drop by drop. This gives them time to think about it. There may be 'politics' attached to who, how, and when you tell others about what you want to do.

Early on, decide how much information you want to share and at what times. Sometimes people respond best to an idea when they have time to warm up to it, especially if they don't understand it or its implications initially. That way you also have a chance to get feedback from them and make modifications.

If you release the wrong information to the wrong person at the wrong time, that person may undermine you by starting unnecessary rumors. All kinds of unexpected backlash may come out of this. Don't go seeking ridicule and rejection.

#

Wisely manage the information flow of your vision. Beware before you share!

Question:

21:1 What are your tendencies when it comes to divulging information? Are you likely to give away too much and if so, how can you remind yourself to keep your secrets?

Action Six▶
Take Action

DAY 22: ACT NOW!

Until now, you have been forming your vision on a conceptual level and hopefully getting ready to develop it. It's time 'to action out of the box' and begin your journey.

Ask yourself of your vision: *what is the first action I will take to achieve my vision and when will I take it?* Don't panic. That first action doesn't have to be a big one. You just have to get the momentum going. Maybe you set up a meeting. Maybe you go to the library or get on the internet and commence research. Maybe you fill out some forms and send them off.

I advise you to do it now. Sooner rather than later. If you let your idea sit there without taking action, then it will either stay inert and useless, or someone else will come along and do it. I ask you: what can you do today, in the next hour? Now? Do it.

If your vision is the most imperative thing you want to accomplish, shouldn't most of your thoughts and actions be focused on achieving it? If your vision is as important and necessary as you have realized it is, why isn't your next action connected to implementing your vision?

#

Get moving!

Questions:

22:1 What is the very next action you will take to start the momentum to achieve your vision?

22:2 When will you do it?

Action Seven ▶
Get the Spiritual Implications

DAY 23: **DISTINCTIVE SERVICE**

Why add the action of comprehending spiritual implications? Because, by knowing the context for your vision, you understand how it fits within the broader theme of service.

When your vision is anchored in a more holistic view of reality, it takes on a higher level of meaning. When you face doubts and barriers as you bring your vision to life, holding fast to these spiritual implications helps you continue.

Here are some principles to help you see the spiritual implications of your vision.

You are created in God's image
In the first chapter of Genesis God is, quite literally, creative. He moves in the midst of a formless space, he speaks, and he creates light. But he doesn't stop there. He starts making things on an immense scale. He creates sky, mountain, humans. He creates a universe of both the seen and the unseen.

We know that humans are unique from the rest of creation in that they are made in God's image. He gave humans the ability to communicate and love, to innovate and create. Because you are created in God's image, that image is the foundation for your identity as a person and as an entrepreneur.

You are created to tend the garden
Your purpose is to care for the world around you, because that is a mandate God has given to all people. This calling originates from the first role given to humans. Early in the book of Genesis it says, "Then the Lord God took the man and put him into the Garden of Eden to cultivate it and keep it." Genesis 2:15. There you have the original job description.

It entails more than cultivating a physical garden. God desires that humans tend to the totality of reality, including the physical, social, economic and spiritual realms

You are called to redeem a broken world
The original mandate of tending the garden is still valid for humans today. But there came along an interfering problem: evil. Because of it, this world is broken and fallen. Because of it, the original mandate expanded.

The good news is that God provided a solution for the inherent evil in the world. He is spiritually and in every other way. At the same time, we are called to live lives of faith in him and bring God's lordship into all areas of life. We are called to care for the fallen world, to restore it into a right relationship with God and make it better. The Bible is rich with examples of this: everything from managing our lives, caring for the poor, repairing social and political systems, spiritual restoration, etc.

This access to God is not passive. It is an active calling to participate with him in that innovation and redemption. We are called to participate with him in redeeming a broken world. Your vision should be within that context.

You are called to inaugurate the kingdom of God
Redeeming the world—restoring and making it better—is required, but it is not the end of the story. It must be seen in the context of inaugurating the kingdom of God. The teachings and acts of Christ are first and foremost about this. Jesus didn't come to earth merely to redeem people but also to announce and enact the arrival of God's long awaited reign.

Your entrepreneurial vision is not God. Your vision is something to be brought before God and then positioned within his reign and kingdom. While it is okay to be highly passionate, even obsessed by your vision, do not let it replace God. Vision is subservient to God and needs to be positioned accordingly. His lordship applies to every corner of your life, including your vision.

You gain personal joy through innovation

Being innovative can provide you with personal joy and fulfillment. This is evident when you observe God's reaction after creating the heavens and the earth. At the end of the first day in which he had made light, God stood back, took a look and saw that it was good. At the end of the sixth day, he saw that all he had made was "very good". Amazingly, because you are created in God's image, you can have a similar sense of satisfaction in your work, that is, in going through the daily challenges of achieving your entrepreneurial idea.

You are holding a unique purpose and vision

The Reformers believed that all professions were noble and contained dignity. Think about the following quotes within the context of your vision.

William Tyndale, the first person to translate the Bible from its original languages into English, and was martyred for it, said, "If we look externally, there is a difference between washing of dishes and preaching the word of God, but as touching to please God, none at all." And Ulrich Zwingli, another Reformer, said, "There is nothing in the universe so like God as the worker."

This means that your vision, as your particular calling, has meaning and dignity before God. Unfortunately, some Christians teach, either implicitly or explicitly, that certain activities or professions are valued more than others. Our purpose is *to cultivate and redeem the world around us*. That means that all occupations (and visions) hold equal dignity when they fulfill this role.

Questions:

23:1 In light of the principles listed above, can you identify specific spiritual implications in your project?

23:2 How do you live your life with redemption in mind?

DAY 24: IN THE SPIRIT

Viewing your project in a spiritual light will help you recall its importance and will continue to motivate you when the stress levels soar, the bills come all at once, and you find yourself wondering if you took the right path.

Review a few considerations with me to firmly position your vision in God's plan for your life.

It's redeeming and transforming
Now that you have formulated a plan and have hopefully even started to implement that plan, revisit your answers to the questions about the redeeming nature of your vision. Can you articulate how your project will not only care for and redeem the world, but also make it better?

It's about your faith
While this goal you have chosen for yourself may make a difference out in the world, what difference will it make for you personally, especially concerning your faith? How is it going to affect your spirituality?

Questions:

24: 1 Now that you have formulated your vision and your plan, can you articulate the redemptive qualities of your vision?

24: 2 How will your faith apply to your vision-journey and how do you expect it to grow? How will it impact your spirituality and faith?

24:3 What does this project truly mean to you personally? Why it is important and what difference will it make in your life?

DAY 25: SUM IT UP

Now, summarize your entrepreneurial project. This is a synopsis composed of brief sentences or bullet points.

Sample Vision Summary

Current Situation: What is my current situation? A brief bio.

Vision: Go back to the vision statement that you wrote in a previous chapter. Think about it and rewrite it if you think it needs to be changed or fine-tuned.

Strategy (Remember, there are two parts.)

1. Personal behaviors to change:

2. Forward plan:

Product: What exactly is my product?

Market: Who is the market for my product?

Production: Where will my product be produced?

Delivery: How is my product distributed or delivered?

Administration: What organization and tools do I need? Do I need partners and what is our agreement? What does each person contribute to the project, and what does each person receive from the project?

Finances: What finances are required and where do they come from?

Targets and Dates: What are my major milestones and by when?

Accountability: To whom will I be accountable?

Spiritual Impact:

Final Assignment:

Go back through your notebook and write a summary of your vision using the above headings. Keep it between one and three pages. It is helpful for you to have your this summary to keep you on track. And this document can provide the base for writing an Executive Summary, which is essential if you are trying to explain your idea to others, and for raising financing.

INTO THE JOURNEY

You've done it. You have identified your deepest desires and narrowed them down to one vital thing you want to happen at a definite point in the near future. You worked hard to assemble the plan and structure to bring your vision to life. To close, here are a few thoughts.

Focus on the vision
Remember that vision is 'a vivid mental picture'. Give it more of your mental space. If your busy life involves many responsibilities, then prioritize them in light of your vision, and commit to doing at least one thing every day that will support your vision.

Stop living solely for your personal pleasure
Don't let yourself get caught in a purely pleasure-seeking cycle that ignores the suffering of those around you. As the greatest commandment said: love the Lord your God and your neighbor as yourself. Remember, a good vision, one that matters, makes things better. It redeems. A good vision changes the system in a positive way.

Re-route the routine
If you travel anywhere in the word you will see people continually performing the routines and patterns valued by their established social systems. Routines are fine—as long as they don't prevent you from making a difference with your life. And routines are especially limiting if they stop you from doing what really matters. If you retire into a secure routine—whether you're twenty or sixty—your wrinkles won't come with much wisdom.

Journey in faith
God is Lord. Step out in faith. May you achieve you achieve your entrepreneurial quest. As you enter the unknown, remember that you will learn as you go along. In the end, things may turn out very differently than you originally envisioned—maybe even better. To conclude;

What is your vision?

You know it.

Now go for it.

About the Author

Dr. Ralph McCall grew up in California and played as a professional basketball player in Israel, Europe, Asia, and Africa. He worked for a subsidiary organization of the World Trade Organization and the United Nations, and then as a manager in Hewlett-Packard, responsible for operations in Europe, Africa and the Middle-East. After leaving HP he worked with business partners in Switzerland with whom he started several companies. He has taught entrepreneurship courses and seminars at universities all over the world, and currently he is the director of several companies in Switzerland.

He has a Bachelor of Science degree from New York State University, an MBA from Henley Management College in the U.K., and a Doctorate in Business Administration from Brunel University in the U.K.

He bases himself in a small village in the Swiss Alps.

About the Workbook

This workbook is a condensed version of the book, Entrepreneur? Bring Your Vision to Life, ISBN 978-0-9759082-9-7. If you go to the Vision to Life website you will find supporting materials, including a free five week group study guide.

The workbook is part of a growing series of guidebooks devoted to helping readers gain new insights into areas of practical living, such as entrepreneurship, ownership, vocation, and other topics. They systematically develop foundational principles, and then present reflective questions that enable you to 'Bring Your Vision to Life.'

For more information go to, www.visiontolife.org

Destinée Media

This is a Destinée Media publication. Destinée aims to bring a fresh perspective to living, culture and worldviews. We publish both fiction and nonfiction, many of our works dealing with themes of theology, spirituality and Christian living.

We thank you for your interest in our materials and hope that you find them both relevant and challenging.

For more information please go to: www.destineemedia.com

www.ingramcontent.com/pod-product-compliance
Lightning Source LLC
Chambersburg PA
CBHW082336300426
44109CB00046B/2508